Hey! A dog.

Draw her a friend.

Create other animals with these sponges.

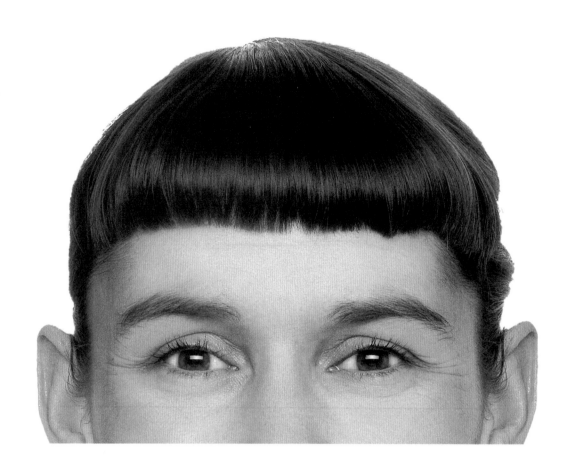

Complete the photos.

Drip, drip, drip. It's raining on the elegant lady.

The chef looks sleepy. He could use a rest.

Who is wearing this hat?

The princess loves to make funny faces.

Watch out! This motorcyclist is irate.

Who is wearing this cap?

Everyone at the party must have a mustache.

Even the girls?

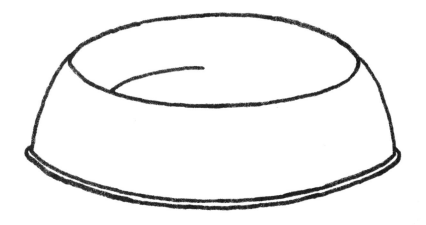

Fill the dog's bowl.

Clouds, birds, airplanes, or UFOs... What do you see in the sky?

Color the gardener and his plants.

A tree in winter: the snow falls and begins to cover everything.

In the spring, small leaves begin to grow.

Color the rooster like the one in the photo.

Turn this sock into a rooster, too.
What does he say to the first rooster?

This is the ballet of fruits and vegetables.

Draw another dancer.

Continue the ballet...

Draw the other cows in the herd.

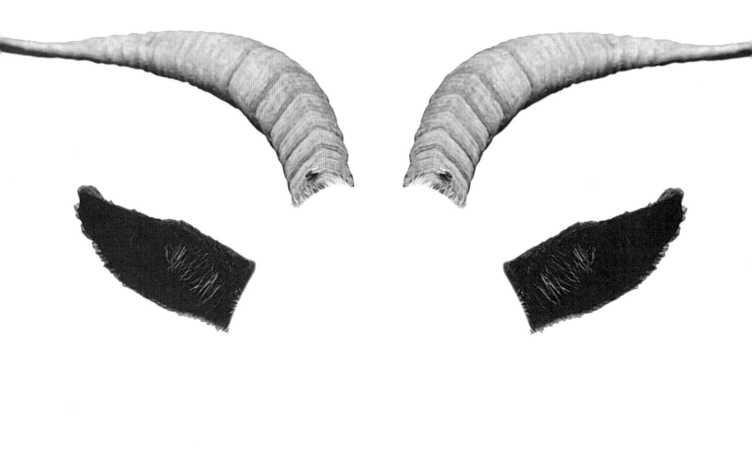

It's a costume party! Finish these outfits.

Recreate the bouquet on the left page in this vase.

This is an unusual vase.

Finish adding flowers to it.

This cup is disguised.

Disguise this cup, too.

Here is the king.

Draw the queen.

Here's a cowboy.

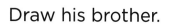

Draw his brother.

Dress up this guy as the Playmobil figure.

What are they telling each other?

Draw them some friends, too.

Disguise the scallop and the shrimp.

What are they saying?

Who are these little rocks?

Draw two monsters.

Imagine their faces.

Draw her shoes.

Who is running behind him?

Who is running in front?   Decorate the sneakers.

All photos by **Jean Tholance**, except:
—The dog, rooster, cow, ears, and horns: Photos by **François Delebecque**
—The bamboo, the blue sky, and trees: Photos by **Ianna Andréadis**

A big thank you to **Florence**, **Laure**, **Arnaud** and **David** for agreeing to pose for this book.
And thank you to **Patrick Couratin** for the finishing touches and good advice.

There are also very beautiful socks from **Tricotage des Vosges** and a magnificent painting by **Jan Frans Van Dael** (1764-1840): *Vase de fleurs, raisins et pêches*, 1810. It is on display in the Louvre. © Photo RMN © Franck Raux.

On page 39 is a famous vase (Vase Savoy, 1936) by Finnish designer **Alvar Aalto** (1898-1976). On the following pages, the very original *vase d'Avril* was created in 1991 by **Tsé-Tsé**.

Also, the Playmobil figure is reproduced with the authorization of **Playmobil®**.
And thank you to **Sam** for the layout.

Pascale Estellon is the author of many books for children, including *Picture This* from Seven Footer Kids.

First published in France under the title *Mon album de photos à dessiner et à colorier* © Editions des Grandes Personnes, 2010.

Published by Seven Footer Kids, an imprint of Seven Footer Press, a division of Seven Footer Entertainment LLC, NY
Manufactured in Shanghai, P.R. China in 07/10
by Stone Sapphire (HK) Limited.
10 9 8 7 6 5 4 3 2

ISBN 978-1-934734-54-4